# WHEN
# Octopods Dream

## a coloring book for everyone

ORIGINAL ILLUSTRATIONS BY

*Laura Medeiros*

Tip:
When using markers,
to prevent the color from bleeding through
to the next design, place a blank sheet
under your page.

# Octopod

*noun*

a cephalopod mollusk from the order Octopoda
this includes octopuses and paper nautiluses
all octpods have eight arms

When Octopods Dream
a coloring book for everyone

©LAURA MEDEIROS

©LAURA MEDEIROS

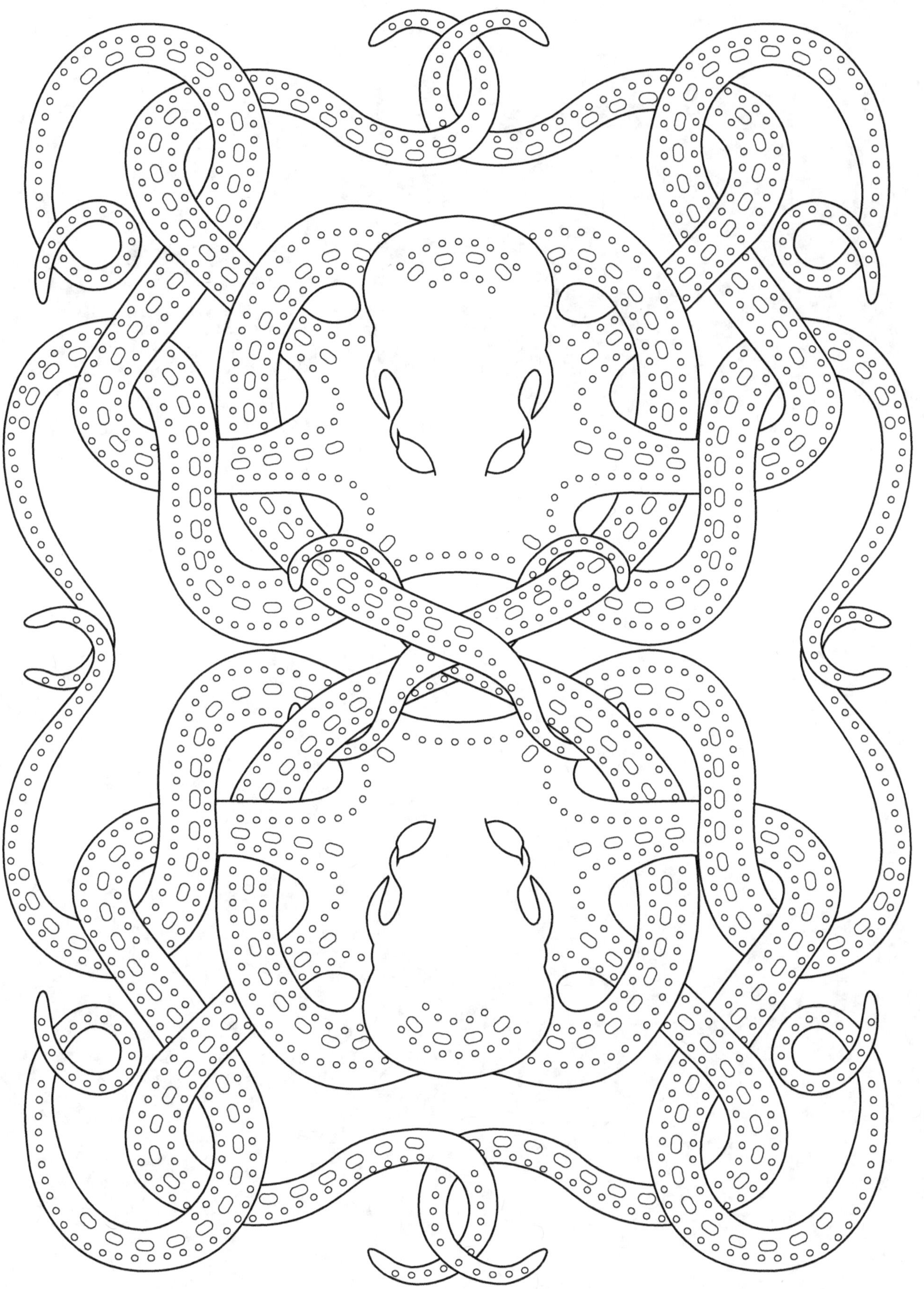

# Coloring Books

### BY

## Laura Medeiros

Unique whimsical coloring books available in print from Amazon.com

and for download from https://www.etsy.com/shop/ColoringwithLaura

# WWW.LAURAMEDEIROS.COM/COLORING-BOOKS